LET'S TALK ABOUT MONEY

A Conversation Guide
for Intentional Communities

Eris Weaver
Cotati, CA

Illustrations: Eris Weaver
Author photo: Karen Preuss

ISBN 978-1-478-14864-7

Table of Contents

ACKNOWLEDGEMENTS

It takes a village to write a book, and this one would not exist without my village, FrogSong. Thirteen years ago, I walked into a Santa Rosa living room and fell in love; like any relationship, it has changed my life in ways I could never have imagined. A particular shout out to Dave Ergo for the germination of these ideas.

To Katie McCamant & Chuck Durrett – I continue to appreciate and be inspired by you! The cohousing movement owes so much to the combination of Chuck's optimism, vision, and genuine love of people with Katie's pragmatism and drive. Thanks also to the facilitators and trainers who have been my teachers, mentors, and colleagues, especially Rob Sandelin, Tree Bressen, Laird Schaub, Annie Russell, Bob Flax, and Lisa Heft. I never would have even thought about writing a book until nudged by my marketing mommies Cynthia Riggs and Roberta Ryan, and my Monday morning accountability partners have kept me moving. Catharine Bramkamp and Stacey Meinzen are responsible for turning my pile of notes and doodles into a REAL BOOK – thanks, gals!

The communities with which I have worked continue to amaze me with their courage and honesty and willingness to get their hands dirty; we are truly a special tribe. Everyone who has ever served as a board member or volunteer with Coho/US (especially Rick Mockler and Grace Kim) has my deepest gratitude and affection.

First and last, forever and always, I couldn't accomplish anything I do without the love and support of my wife Leslie Warren.

INTRODUCTION

Many communities find themselves in conflict over financial and budget issues... and the current economic situation doesn't help! Conflicts about money are really conflicts about values. This workbook is designed to help your community have useful conversations about your financial values - conversations that lead to greater understanding and connection as well as more effective financial decision-making.

This book started out as a workshop I designed with my friend and colleague David Ergo, a financial recovery counselor, for the 2009 National Cohousing Conference in Seattle, WA. The audience included members of forming and established cohousing communities from all over the United States and Canada.

The idea germinated out of a conversation Dave and I had after I'd worked with several communities who were stuck in conflict about financial issues. We discussed how taboo it is in our culture to talk about money – we talk more about our sexual histories and activities than we do our financial status. This holds true even in our intentional communities – we discuss our values around parenting, the environment, etc. but don't think to explore our money values until we find ourselves stuck or in conflict about a budget, membership dues, or a particular expenditure.

After leading the workshop several times in various settings, I first put it into workbook form to give a particular group the opportunity to work with our exercises and ideas without having my having to travel to be in the same room with them. While using an outside facilitator can offer many advantages, not every community can afford to bring one in whenever there is a conflict or a stuck place. The included workshop outline is obviously generic, lacking the customization that is part of working face-to-face; if you have purchased the optional phone consultation, I can help your community's facilitator(s) tweak the agenda to meet your specific needs. You can run the entire workshop in one day, or use the various exercises individually over time.

I look forward to feedback about how well this works for you!

Throughout the book I have included case studies – stories I've witnessed from real communities addressing real issues. In order to protect my clients' confidentiality, I have changed identifying information and in some cases collapsed multiple events into one story.

Case Study: The Last Dollar

I first started thinking about this whole issue of money and values because of a confusing situation I observed in my own community. We are fairly affluent, having moved in with over half a million dollars in the bank for capital improvements. Over the years we've agreed to allocate various amounts for money for various projects – a hot tub, a playground, finishing out a second story in the workshop, etc. Our enthusiasm for thinking up projects was greater than our ability to actually get the projects completed; we might agree to fund a project that didn't actually get implemented for a year or more.

At one point Ted and Jennie (names have been changed for privacy) suggested spending a good chunk of money on installing photovoltaic panels throughout the property, making us electrically self-sufficient. No one doubted that this was in keeping with our community's deepest, most cherished environmental values. The amount estimated for the project was sizeable, about a third of the original account balance. Debbie and Randy blocked the allocation because it might use up the last of that original pot of money.

"What if we spend all our money and then next year we realize we want or need something else? We won't have anything left!"

To them it was obvious that you don't spend the last of your savings. To Ted and Jennie it seemed obvious that spending money on something that would save us money in the long term was the most judicious thing to do. They pointed to other pots of money within the community and argued that we could always work to raise money later for something else we wanted. Debbie and Randy were un-swayed by this line of reasoning; it just wasn't responsible or prudent to allocate The Last Dollar.
This discussion obviously touched on individuals' feelings about security; how much one needs to have in savings in order to feel secure; optimism about future fundraising capacities and varying degrees of comfort with risk. It really had nothing to do with the actual project itself, which everyone really wanted.

It's so easy to think that the only reason people fight about money is because they don't have enough of it. Here was a community that by many standards had much more than enough, but was still embroiled in conflict. I realized then how much our community conversations about finances were really about our underlying values.

HOW TO USE THIS WORKBOOK

The agenda on the next page reflects the original three to four hour workshop, which was structured for an audience made up of members of multiple communities. The sequencing of exercises was designed to move from shallow to deep, and from personal to collective. Feel free to add, drop, or rearrange exercises to meet your community's current needs!

ORIGINAL WORKSHOP AGENDA

After this workshop, participants will:

- Have a deeper understanding of the connection between money & values
- Learn new tools they can use in their communities' conversations about money
- Begin to explore some of their own values about money

TIME	ACTIVITY	PAGE
15 min.	INTRODUCTION • Goals, ground rules, logistics • Any other opening activities typically expected by your group	na
15 min.	TOOLS FOR CONVERSATIONS ABOUT MONEY/VALUES • Kinetic mapping	16
15 – 30 min.	SHELTER SCALES	18
15 min.	EXAMINING PERSONAL MONEY VALUES • "Big question" brainstorm	23
40 – 60 min.	PERSONAL MONEY HISTORY (dyads or triads)	24
10 – 20 min.	BREAK	na
40 – 60 min.	• Necessity vs. luxury (small groups) • Winning the lottery (small groups)	25
15 – 30 min.	EXPLORING SHARED COMMUNITY VALUES • Case studies • Review shared vision / values	30
20 min.	TOOLS FOR RANKING & PRIORITIZING • Dot Voting • Binary Comparison; Importance/Time Sensitivity Matrix	36
10 – 20 min.	EVALUATION & CLOSING	na

ADAPTING THE AGENDA

In adapting this agenda for use with your specific community and the question(s) you are currently exploring, I suggest:

- Moving the use of shelter scales to the later section on Exploring Community Values, revising the questions to fit your specific needs.
- Many of the Tools for Ranking & Prioritizing may already be familiar to the group and thus may not need to be reviewed. Depending upon your current specific need, it may be appropriate to choose one or more and use it to explore that current question. The section on Exploring Community Values is a likely place for expansion.
- Any of the other exercises can be expanded or contracted by changing the amount of debriefing time, debriefing in small groups versus large group, etc.

GET CREATIVE!

Feel free to use these ideas as a springboard to designing your own exercises and activities. Every community – and every facilitator! – has their own style. Think about your desired outcome for each exercise; the overall emotional tone you're trying to create; and what you already know about the kinds of activities and language with which your group is familiar.

Case Study: Designing a Values Exercise

I once worked with a group of others to design an exercise to help a community clarify their shared values. The group already had brainstormed list of values, and the next step was to find out which ones they shared the most deeply. Another facilitator suggested using the Dot Voting exercise on page 36.

As the group was looking to share deeply, we were trying for a serious and ceremonial tone that would foster that kind of emotional connection. "Voting" on values just didn't feel right. We kept checking our language during the discussion – we weren't asking the group to "vote" whether they "liked" a listed value, we were after how deeply they hold that value compared to others. What image might create and reinforce that idea? Eventually we hit it: concentric circles rather than lists! That might get people out of their left-brain, logical mind and more into the right-brain, value- and emotion-driven mental space that we were after. Each value would be written on a sheet of paper with concentric circles, and each individual would mark each sheet based on how deeply they held that value: in the center if it was core, and farther out if it wasn't. Oh, we were feeling brilliant now!

As we kept discussing how to structure the exercise, using the sticky dots that the group had used for other exercises wasn't feeling exactly right. The dots still had a voting connotation, not to mention a connection with office supplies – still not the mood we were after. Someone suggested, how about a thumbprint? Someone else excitedly went on a scavenger hunt for some ink pads. How much more individual and personal and physically connected could you get than marking your values using your THUMB?

The whole activity proceeded as well as we had anticipated. Would this have worked for every community? Of course not. Some might have found it too "touchy-feely." My point in sharing this story is as an example of how you might come up with your own unique version of these exercises!

TOOLS FOR CONVERSATIONS ABOUT MONEY

KINETIC MAPPING

Kinetic mapping is a fun, physical, get-'em-up-and-moving activity that allows you to get a quick overview of how widely a list of values or ideas are shared within the group.

For each question, indicate two opposite ends of the room as representing two polar opposites and imagine a line running between them. Ask participants to physically put themselves in a space along the continuum that represents their current opinion. They may stand all the way to one extreme, smack dab in the middle if they are neutral or mixed, or anywhere else along the continuum. (It's OK if they are bunched up, they don't have to stand literally just on the line!) After everyone's taken their place, stop and notice the pattern.

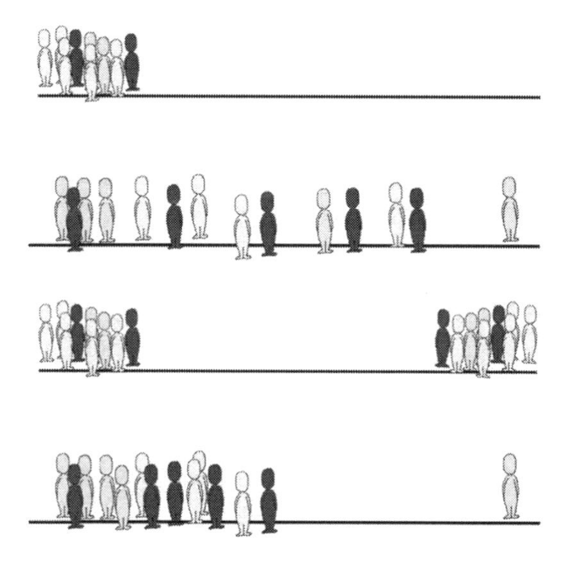

Is everyone all clumped up together in one general area? That indicates a lot of congruent thinking in the group.

If everyone is fairly evenly distributed, it may be a challenge to find a solution that works for everyone.

The most polarized distribution – two camps at opposite ends. (This has actually been rare, in my experience.)

Everyone is clumped with one or two outliers at another end – care must be taken not to let the outliers be scapegoated.

MAPPING THE MONEY

Here are some useful kinetic mapping questions about money. Feel free to create and add your own!

- I'm happy/comfortable with how much money I earn
- I'm happy/comfortable with how much money I save
- I'm happy/comfortable with how much money our community has
- I'm happy/comfortable with our community dues
- If something needs to be fixed, I favor doing ourselves vs. hiring it out

- If I buy something, I go for cheapest (regardless of value) vs. highest quality (regardless of cost)
- I'm a saver vs. I'm a spender
- I track all my expenditures & reconcile my accounts regularly vs. I have no clue how much I have

SHELTER SCALES

Shelter scales offer an opportunity to anonymously gather sensitive information that individuals may not feel comfortable sharing out loud with the whole group, but is necessary for decision-making purposes. My observation has been that, after the debrief, many folks end up disclosing the previously hidden information – seeing others' information and discussing it in a supportive and caring way often melts any resistance to sharing information.

Each participant is given a sticky note or slip of paper for each question and asked to write their answer on it. Do one question at a time – state the question, give folks time to write, and then collect the notes, sticking them up on the flip-chart or wall and clustering them in patterns that make sense.

Questions usually fall into two types. One is just a simple number : How much can I afford to contribute to this project? The other is a number along a five-point

Likkert scale: On a scale of 1-5, how much do you agree with this statement? (1=strongly disagree, 2=somewhat disagree, 3=neutral, 4=somewhat agree, 5=strongly agree). The more clearly the question is stated, the better!

Some sample shelter scale questions include:

- How much am I willing and able to pay for a house?
- How much am I willing and able to pay for monthly dues?
- What percentage of my income do I save?
- What is my household's monthly income?

Here is an example of using a shelter scale with a forming community that was seeking land, and stating very strongly that their project needed to be "affordable." Affordability is interpreted and experienced very differently by different people! Each member was asked to write on a sticky note the highest amount they would be willing and able to pay for their home in cohousing. These were clustered on the flipchart; most were clustered in a fairly close range. We could now see that, for this particular group of people at this time, an "affordable" home price for most was around $185K.

$195K

$120K $190K $200K $250K

$185K $195K

Case Study: Affordability

"Affordability" has got to be one of the most emotion-laden words in the development process! Everyone wants home prices to be affordable, which I think generally means "affordable to ME." Of course, what is affordable to one household may be very different than what seems affordable to another. There are formulas that realtors and mortgage companies use to determine what a household can "afford" based on their income, but this doesn't touch the emotional content of the word. For someone to feel that they can afford something, they must weigh it against not just their income, but their other expenses, and how they FEEL about their income, their other expenses, and their priorities. Two households with the same number of people and the same income may have a very different idea about what home price they can afford.

I worked with one community in a rural, economically depressed area. The members had entered into an agreement with a developer and given him some parameters about the price points they desired, the density (number of houses per acre) they found acceptable, etc. The developer then looked at the property, its purchase price, and estimated construction costs, and came up with a pro forma. He saw his task as calculating what could realistically be built on the property. The group was very unhappy with his estimates, because both the density and the price of the homes were higher than they wished.

I led the community members through the shelter scale exercise. The prices that the group members could afford were considerably lower than what the developer felt could realistically be built. The group was frustrated at having spent money on this consultant to find that not only could they not afford to build on this property, but that they couldn't afford to build at all! Not only were they were despondent at the loss of their dream, they could not see an alternative way to create the community they so wanted. Perhaps if they had done this exercise earlier in their process, before engaging the developer's services, they could have used the Out of the Box exercise (page 33) to come up with solutions to their goal (live in community) that were outside of the box (build from scratch) – mobile homes? share a big existing house?

Another group from a wealthy suburb of San Francisco were discussing their dreams for cohousing, and also used the word "affordable." These folks had professional jobs and had built considerable equity in the large homes they'd owned for twenty to thirty years. We worked through the shelter scale exercise to determine what they could afford. Their concept of affordability was thousand of dollars higher and the prices were orders of magnitude larger than those of the rural community.

Every time I've shared this exercise with a group, there have been a few members whose numbers were outliers – significantly higher or lower than the center around which the majority clustered. Folks with higher financial assets can certainly remain with the group, although they may decide they wish to align with a community that can afford more costly features in their commons. What is more challenging is figuring out how much to accomodate folks whose "affordability factor" is significantly lower than the majority. Does that household need to drop out? This can be heartbreaking, if they are beloved, hard-working, integral members of the community. Should the entire group lower costs in an attempt to include that household? What kind of resentment might they experience if they do so, only to have that household still drop out later?

For these reasons, it is crucial for forming communities to answer the affordability question as early as possible, and clearly communicate the resulting home price estimates to prospective members. It is far better to deal with this issue, allowing prospective members to select in or out based on affordability early on, than to bid a tearful "good-bye" to a member who has worked with the group for months or years.

EXAMINING PERSONAL MONEY VALUES

"BIG QUESTION" BRAINSTORMS

For each of these questions, ask for participants to brainstorm. Remind them that the point of a brainstorm is to fling the ideas out, not to evaluate or elaborately explain them. Scribe them on a flipchart so you can refer back to them in the debrief. Use a separate sheet for each questions.

- "What is money?"
- "What sayings about money have you heard?"
- If you had to come up with a short phrase or slogan to describe your personal approach to money, what would it be?
- For a group that has been together awhile: If you had to come up with a short phrase or slogan to describe our community's approach to money, what would it be?

When the answers to one question start to run down, don't be afraid to sit with silence for a few beats – often more thoughts will begin to bubble out, especially from those who don't think and speak as quickly as others.

After it does seem like all ideas have been captured for a particular question, take a moment to debrief – What stands out? Do you see any patterns? Does any of this surprise you? Did you learn something about yourself or somebody else?

PERSONAL MONEY HISTORY

Ask participants to form dyads or triads, depending upon the size of the group and how much time you want to allot for this exercise. Invite them to take turns sharing their memories and experiences about money growing up, and how that has shaped their current lives.

The appendix includes a Money Autobiography, a lengthy list of questions that should be given to participants in advance. You could also hand them out for reference during this exercise, or post some of the questions on a flipchart.

It can be helpful to ring a bell or otherwise mark time divisions for folks to switch who is speaking. Be sure and give this exercise enough time! Initial shares generally start on the surface, and it takes awhile for folks to settle in and feel comfortable going deeper.

After making sure that everyone has had a turn to share, bring the whole group back together. I generally don't suggest a long report-out after small group exercises like this, because I think it can inhibit the intimacy and disclosure that is the whole reason for doing it in a small versus a large group. However, folks often feel unsatisfied if there isn't some kind of whole group debrief. Rather than going around group by group, I ask for individual comments "popcorn" style. I ask folks NOT to disclose other people's information without their permission, but to share their overall revelations or discoveries:

Did you experience any moments of
"Wow!" or
"Aha!" or
"Oh, shit!" or
"Hmm"?

NECESSITY/LUXURY

Depending upon their social class, family dynamics, personalities, and priorities, people often have different perceptions about what possessions and/or experiences they classify as necessities and which they classify as luxuries. When money is tight, this can be an area that is ripe for conflict if the group hasn't gotten clarity beforehand. This exercise offers an opportunity for folks to look at how they categorize and prioritize when financial resources are limited.
In the Appendix is a sheet that has two lists, one for individual- or family-owned items and one for community-owned items. (Feel free to make additions or sub-

tractions to the list that make sense for your particular community.) Participants are asked to make a checkmark to indicate which items they personally perceive as necessities and which are luxuries.

Ask participants to do the exercise first by themselves silently. This may be followed by small-group discussion; alternately, you could do a whole-group discussion, focusing on the second list of community-owned items. It can be particularly intriguing to notice when people put the same item as luxury on one list and necessity on the other.

Case Study: Running Water: Necessity or Luxury?

When I created this exercise, I used items that had been issues of controversy in some groups I'd worked with and some that were seen as "no brainers" – items that EVERYONE in the group would assume were necessary accoutrements of daily life. Most of these groups were solidly middle class urban or suburban homeowners. Cars (for adults), computers, televisions, etc. were owned by everyone. Travel, private schools for children, cars (for teenagers), second homes were within reach of many, but not all, members. Education, art, beauty, personal fulfillment, and connection with the larger world were among their key values. Most members of these groups automatically assumed that their common house would contain beautiful flooring, new furniture, matching dinnerware, etc.

When using the exercise with an intentionally low-tech, poor, rural community, they laughed – matching plates? Their conflicts were over whether they should have electricity or running water! Their community value of voluntary simplicity, combined with their low incomes and the undeveloped state of their property, meant that they had a very different relationship to consumer goods than the previous groups.

The other issue that comes up in this exercise has to do with the money versus time continuum. There are always some group members who prefer doing something themselves versus hiring it out. This is sometimes about lowering costs, but it also has to do with values of self-reliance; enjoyment of the work itself; and a belief in community-building through shared work.

While the list of which specific goods and services will vary hugely between groups, the common thread is that ALL of us have choices about how and where we spend our money. We all make priorities, and categorize some expenditures are necessities for our well-being and happiness while others are desired luxuries. The differences lie in where we draw that line.

In order to customize the lists for your specific group, choose some items that appear to be no brainers and others that are somewhat out of reach for many members. A ratio of around 50/50 is good.

WINNING THE LOTTERY

The previous exercise looks at priorities when resources are scarce; this exercise asks participants to think from a place of abundance.

Each individual is handed a large amount of money, which they have just won in a lottery. They are asked to make a list detailing what they would do with it – save it, spend it, etc. I generally use $100K as the amount – it is big enough to feel fairly luxurious, but not so big that it is out of the realm of imagining, the way that $1 million might be. Feel free to change the number if it makes more sense for your group's socioeconomic status.

I like to use play money – raid the Monopoly game or get play money from a store that sells party favors. It makes it a little more fun, but also gets to the kinesthetic learners and the doers in a way that just an abstract number doesn't.

After everyone has completed their list done, tell them that, whoops, taxes will take half of it away! Now they have to narrow down their list.

A third question is to imagine that the community as a whole has been gifted the $100K, rather than just the individual.

Again, debriefing can be done in small groups or as a whole group.

- If you won $100K, what would you do with it?
- Oops, taxes are going to take away half ($50K) of your prize! How do you feel about that? What would you ditch on your original list?
- If I gave your community $100K, how would you invest it? What would you do with it?

EXPLORING SHARED MONEY VALUES

This is the section that is most ripe for customizing to your community's current issues and needs. If you purchased the optional telephone consultation session, we can use it to discuss the best methods for clarifying and working with your community's current issue. Most financial conflicts in intentional communities seem to fall into one of the following categories:

- Some of us want to spend money on X and others don't. This frequently surfaces when the product or service is one that will be used by a subset of community members: children's play structure; a treadmill; a piano.
- Some of us want to spend more money on Y than others do. What level of quality, aesthetics, etc. are we willing to pay for?
- Some of us want to do Z ourselves, while others want to spend money hiring it out. Cohousers are do-it-yourselfers!
- We have more things that we want to spend money on than we have money, so we need to prioritize the list. (I can't think of a single aggregation of people for whom this isn't an issue.)
- We need more money in the group coffers, but some of us are unwilling or unable to contribute more. (The more diverse your community is economically, the more likely it is to experience this issue.)

Connecting Specific Expenditures to Specific Values

Budgeting and financial decisions are values-based, whether those values have been made explicit or not. The more work the group has done in clarifying common goals and values, the more easily financial values can be connected to those common values.

- Have your current values statement posted on a wall or chart, or hand out copies.
- Write up the expenditure or decision that is currently vexing the group.
- For each item on the values list, ask the question, "How does [the issue] connect to [this value]?"

- Scribe the ideas suggested in two columns, + for those in which the proposed expenditure affirms the value and – for those in which it seems contrary to that value. This can be a helpful way to visualize all of the competing ideas/ arguments/concerns.

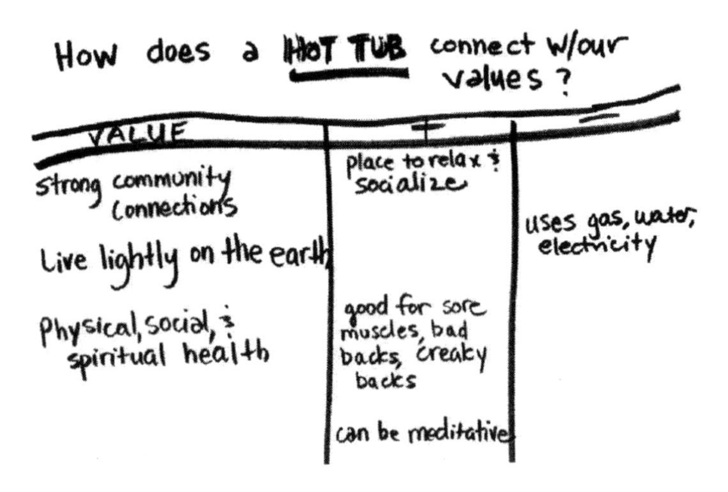

If you are not working on a specific current issue, or don't have well-defined community values, you can still use a variation of this exercise to surface members' values individual values.

- Ask participants to think of a community expenditure that they had a strong feeling about; either congruent with or contrary to one of their values. Write it on a sticky note, along with the value that was invoked. Add a + if it affirmed one that values or a – if it was in conflict with that value.

- Stick 'em all up. Cluster the results and look for patterns. Note common items, especially those with BOTH a + and a -.

WE CAN'T THINK OUTSIDE THE BOX IF WE DON'T KNOW WHICH BOX WE'RE TRAPPED IN

Often our groups get stuck when we think we have considered every possible solution, none of which seem workable. In order to come up with new ideas, we have to take a moment to realize what box we're stuck trapped in. Here's an exercise to help you recognize the box so you can think outside of it!

- Have all of your suggested options up on a flip chart.
- Look and see if you can find something that they ALL HAVE IN COMMON.
- THAT is your box! (Or at least ONE of your boxes! There may be more than one.) Now, move to a brainstorm of possible solutions that do NOT share that characteristic. Go ahead and let it get silly if necessary.
- If nothing on that list seems workable, repeat – what do all of those solutions have in common? Now brainstorm outside of THAT box. Repeat as necessary.

(This exercise can be done in a lot of situations – it is fun, stimulates creativity, both of which community building!)

Case Study: Fixing the Roof

A retrofit community was struggling with the need to finance extensive building repairs – leaking roofs needed fixing before the rainy season, etc. They did not have enough money in the bank and someone suggested a special assessment to fund the repairs. However, several members had recently lost jobs and were already at the financial breaking point, unable to contribute any more money. The residents felt very stuck.

The group tried to brainstorm other solutions, including setting up a way for members with more assets to lend money to those who couldn't afford an assessment right now. While the lower-income members appreciated the sentiment, they were understandably unwilling to take on additional debt.

As group members worked through this exercise, it became clear that their unspoken assumption – their box – was that in any cash call, all members must contribute equally. They placed high a value on equality and fairness and it had never occurred to them that they could consider unequal financial contributions. Once that was stated out loud, they began to discuss what the situation could look like if they let go of that idea. We then used the shelter scale tool. Each household was given a slip of paper and asked to answer the following question with a dollar amount:

How much of your personal money would you be willing and able to contribute to the repairs, without resentment or repayment, regardless of how much anyone else contributes?

When we collected the slips, the amounts ranged from zero to over a thousand dollars. We totalled up all the amounts, and it was more than enough to fund the needed repairs! Those who felt stress over their financial situation were very moved by the generosity of those who had more and were willing to contribute more, for the benefit of all.

TOOLS FOR RANKING & PRIORITIZING

Often when a community is working out a budget, they find that there are more projects and supplies desired than there are dollars to pay for them. So prioritizing and ranking the list becomes important. There are many different tools to help with this task, some of which are better for some categories of decisions than others.

Dot Voting is a quick way to get a sense of how people are thinking. It is good for situations where there is not a lot of "heat" around any of the items on the list; where the outcome is not hugely important; where getting things done quickly is important; or as a "first cut" before using another process. It is a type of voting, so if your group uses consensus you may need an intermediary step before taking action.

Give everyone in the room several sticky dots (or you can use a marker) and ask them to place them on the items that they believe to be the highest priority. How many dots? I suggest using a number that is about one quarter to one third of the total number of items – so if the list has twelve items, give each person three or four dots.

You may want to first discuss criteria for evaluating items. A sample question might be "A good idea or solution would have the following characteristics ...." This can help ensure that everyone is at least thinking about the same outcomes as they go about their ranking.

There will always be someone who asks if they can put all their dots on one item. I usually discourage this because it gives too much weight to individuals with a strong, single agenda. I also ask folks to think about their preferences before sending them up to the board, because some folks will wait and see what everyone else does first.

Usually in this exercise, a few items will rise clearly to the top. You can then decide to focus discussion on those items.

BINARY COMPARISON

It can be difficult to try to rank a long list of things – this technique involves only looking at two items at a time. It takes longer than dot voting, but allows for greater discussion and finesse as the group must agree on each step.

Write each item on a separate sticky note

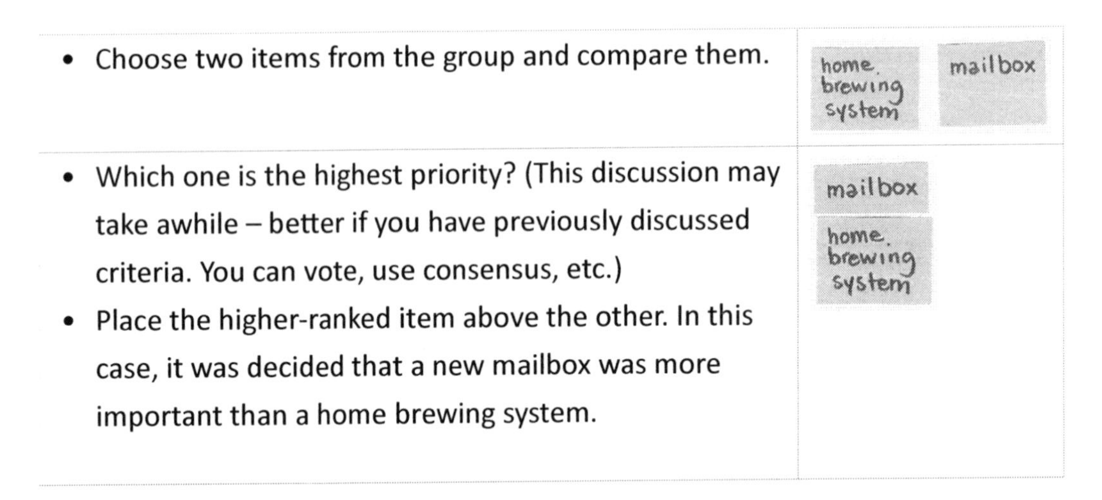

• Choose two items from the group and compare them.	home brewing system / mailbox
• Which one is the highest priority? (This discussion may take awhile – better if you have previously discussed criteria. You can vote, use consensus, etc.) • Place the higher-ranked item above the other. In this case, it was decided that a new mailbox was more important than a home brewing system.	mailbox home brewing system

- Pick a third item and compare it to the one on the bottom – which is higher?
- Is the water heater more important than the brewing system?
- If not, put it at the bottom.
- If it is move it and compare it to the next item up.
- In this example, it was decided that the water heater was more important than the brewing system.

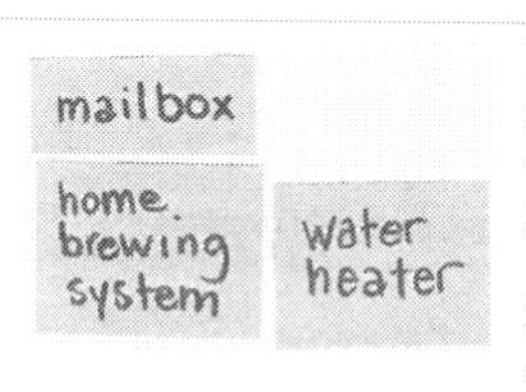

- Keep moving up and comparing the new item to the next item up.
- Is the water heater more important than a mailbox? If not, put it in between the two and stop.
- If it is, move it up to the top.

mailbox
home brewing system
water heater

- In this example, the water heater was deemed more important than the mailbox.
- Continue with new items until they've all been used up!

water heater
mailbox
home brewing system

NEED/WANT/DREAM

This is similar to the luxury/necessity exercise earlier. When subgroups or committees are proposing budgets, or when you are coming up with a list of criteria for an expenditure, you can break characteristics down by the categories of Need, Want, and Dream.

For example, a group may be discussing remodeling and repairs to the Common House, and one issue is flooring. They may decide that they need to replace the kitchen floor (people are tripping on the peeling edges), and want to replace the living room carpet because it has several large stains. Characteristics of the kitchen floor may be:

New kitchen floor

NEED	WANT	DREAM
durable easy-to clean non-toxic under $1500	locally-produced materials "green" materials	beautiful colorful purple?

Case study: Need/Want/Dream budgeting

Jellyfish Creek has incorporated the need/want/dream concept into their annual budgeting process. Each committee or program area submits its budget request to the larger community using this format. Prior to adopting this plan, the annual budget process would come to a standstill over a single line item that someone found unnecessary or otherwise problematic. (Kinda like congressional budgets!) Now it is easy for the community to quickly approve essential expenditures. Items on the dream list can be discussed later at leisure, without holding up the entire budget process up.

TIME/IMPORTANCE MATRIX

The Time/Importance Matrix is a prioritizing system that I use most frequently when planning agendas, strategic planning, and creating action plans, but it could also be useful when comparing different financial issues – for example, prioritizing a list of different maintenance and repair tasks.

Items are compared on two scales: time sensitivity and importance.

I define time sensitivity in this way: if we don't make a decision or take action very soon, something bad will happen. Alternately, if we don't make a decision or take action very soon, we will miss out on something very good.

An issue's importance is defined by your own value system: items that are more deeply connected to the community's most deeply held values and goals are more important.

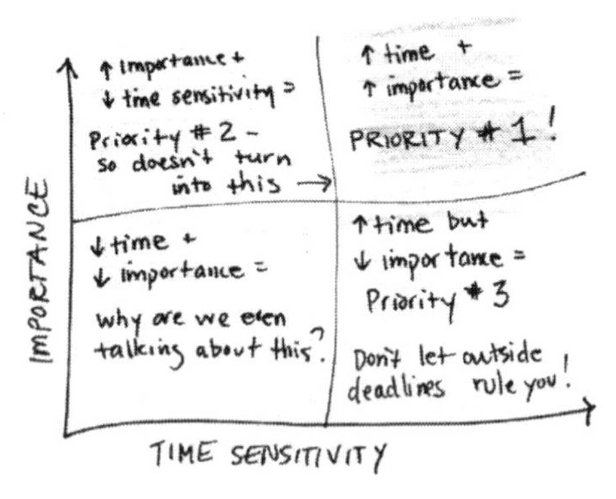

Take some time sorting all of your items into these four quadrants or categories:

1. High importance, high time sensitivity
2. High importance, low time sensitivity
3. Low importance, high time sensitivity
4. Low importance, low time sensitivity

It is usually pretty clear that issues that are high in both importance and time sensitivity should be tackled first. While it should be clear that issues low in both metrics should be put on the back burner or even dropped entirely, groups can often waste a lot of time talking about items in this category if they happen to have a persuasive champion.

The sticky part is prioritizing items that are high in importance but low in time sensitivity, versus those that are low in importance but high in time sensitivity. It is very easy to be swayed by a sense of urgency regarding issues with some kind of time deadline, even if they are not that critically important; and it is also really easy to ignore or neglect very important issues if they do not have a time deadline. Therefore I recommend prioritizing high in importance /low time sensitivity OVER low importance/ high time sensitivity.

For example, imagine that the maintenance committee is trying to prioritize which of a list of tasks to tackle first this Saturday. The roof has a leak and the rainy season will be upon us soon. Some of the gardeners have requested that we purchase and plant more bulbs. The gutters need to be cleared of leaves. And one vocal member is keen to repaint the kitchen.

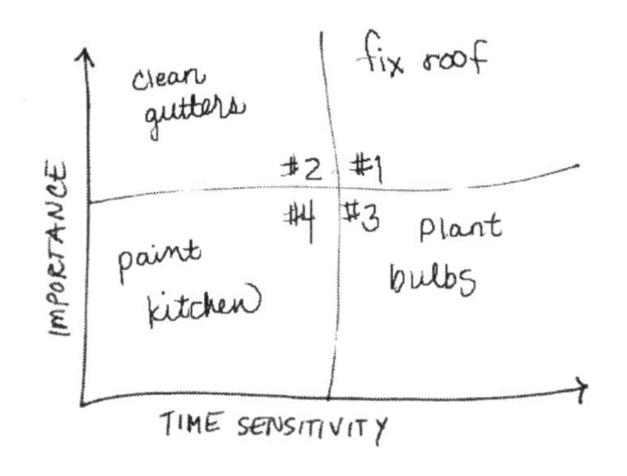

Because it is both time sensitive (rain coming soon) and important (rain indoors isn't fun), fixing the roof will fall into Quadrant 1.

Planting bulbs may have some time sensitivity – you have to do it at a particular time of year - but nothing really important is dependent upon it getting done at all, so we'll put it into Quadrant 3.

Cleaning the gutters doesn't really have to be done right away, but if it doesn't get done eventually it will cause problems later in the year, so it goes into Quadrant 2.

The group decides that painting the kitchen goes into Quadrant 4; it was just painted a year ago and while the color turned out not quite as beautiful as hoped, it is satisfactory.

TOOLS FOR VISUALIZING FINANCIAL DATA

Case Study: Putting Things In Perspective

Long ago in graduate library school, I was introduced to the 80/20 rule: 80% of our reference questions would be answered using 20% of our collection. I've since found the 80/20 rule applicable in many other realms of life, from business (80% of revenues come from 20% of clients) to healthcare utilization (80% of healthcare expenditures are spent on 20% of patients) to criminology (80% of crimes are committed by 20% of criminals). This rule applies to our community conversations about money.

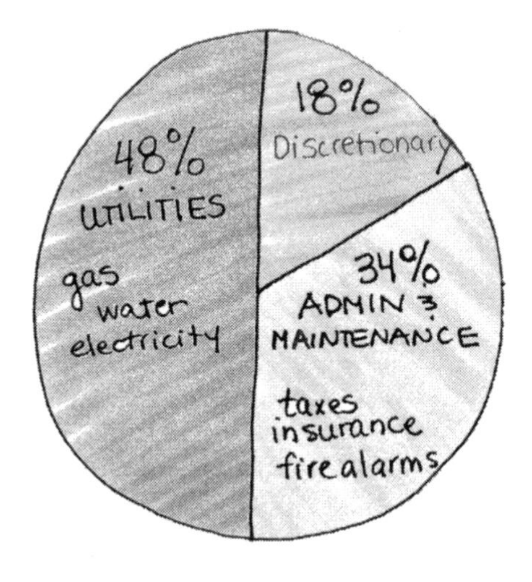

As one of my communities was going through our annual budgeting process one year, I was primarily paying attention to which line items were particularly controversial...and how big a slice of our total budgetary pie was represented by those items. The greatest debate was generated by some of the smallest items. Within the 18% of the total budget devoted to discretionary items, just a handful were particularly hot.

There was little discussion of the biggest chunks – utilities, maintenance, insurance – many of which tend to be seen as fixed costs. Folks tend to focus their attention on the areas over which they feel they have the most control. External costs like utilities and insurance seem out of our control. In addition, the items that fall into that discretionary slice are some of the things that we most value about community life: social events, art, children's play equipment, etc.

Annual budget conversations can be intimidating to those who suffer from math anxiety; large numbers can be hard for some folks to wrap their minds around. In one session it was helpful to remind folks of the fact that $1,000 in the total budget translated to $2.78 of each household's monthly dues.

Budgeting requires using both our left brains (logic and numbers) and our right brains (values and emotions). Presenting financial data in a visual way can help the group put things in perspective, utilizing both methods of thinking simultaneously. Preparing pie charts like the one above, either on flip charts or digitally, can be extremely useful.

Another visualization that we have used was a brilliantly orchestrated spreadsheet, with one large box labeled monthly dues; this was projected on the wall during the meeting. Every change in income or expenses anywhere in the budget was immediately reflected in that box. This made it easy for participants to see how every item accepted, amended, or rejected contributed to monthly dues – which are the end result that most people care about.

CONCLUSION

Case Study: FrogSong's Last Dollar

Let's return to FrogSong's discussion of photovoltaic panels and the controversy over spending The Last Dollar. We had several conversations over several months to explore the issue and try to come to some resolution; even those who didn't want to spend The Last Dollar really wanted to install the panels, but their desire for financial security needed to met in order for them to approve such a large expenditure. Our Finance Committee and Facilitators worked together to structure conversations designed to get at the values underlying all the different sides of the argument; we also brainstormed other ways to raise and save money for other future capital improvements.

As that fiscal year came to a close, we found that we had a budget surplus. We created two new funds – a Project Fund and a Conservation Fund – and a system for depositing money into these accounts. If we come in under budget on utilities (water, electricity, gas, etc.) in any given year, that surplus goes into the Conservation Fund. If we have any other net surplus at the end of the year, we deposit a percentage of it into the Project Fund. So far, we have had a budget surplus every year since we moved in 2003. As these two funds grow each year, the folks who had concerns about spending the original funds have been able to relax – they saw that we ARE indeed able as a community to come up with other funding. We finally did come to consensus on installing the photovoltaic panels. They've not been installed yet due to some state regulatory issues that are in flux; in the meantime, the interest grows and we are poised to start the work as soon as we get the state go-ahead.

By now, I hope that your and your community not only understand the need to have these value-based discussions, but have begun to do so and thus started to get to know each other better and make better financial decisions.

One question I am asked frequently about these exercises – indeed I am asked this about ANY exercise I suggest about any potential controversial issue – is "What if it doesn't work and there is still controversy?"
Or "We tried X and it was still really difficult to make a decision!"

I don't promise that any of these tools will prove to be a Magic Wand. Differences of opinion about money – as well as any other community "hotspot" like parenting, work participation, pets, etc. – are not problems to be solved or fixed once and for all. They are part of the ongoing dance of community. My goal is not to fix problems, but to help your community members dance together more gracefully, step on each other's toes less frequently, and most importantly, HAVE MORE FUN together!

APPENDIX: HANDOUTS TO COPY

LUXURY/NECESSITY

Feel free to add items to this list. Do leave a few blank lines, so that participants can add additional items if they wish. Make enough copies for each participant to have one. You may choose to put the community items on the other side of the page from the personal items.

MONEY AUTOBIOGRAPHY

This handout is best used as pre-work – send it out to participants before the workshop so that they have time to do some reflection on their personal experiences, feelings, and values. It doesn't hurt to have some extra copies the day of the workshop as a prompt for those who did not look at it beforehand.

NECESSITY OR LUXURY?

For each item, check whether you view it as a necessity or a luxury for yourself & your family:

	Necessity	**Luxury**
Dishes that match		
A car		
A dishwasher		
Private school		
Microwave		
Separate bedrooms for the kids		
Garage		
Organic food		

For each item, check whether you view it as a necessity or a luxury for your community:

	Necessity	**Luxury**
Dishes that match		
A dishwasher		
Microwave		
Hot tub		
Guest room		
Swimming pool		
Carport		
Organic food		
Party decorations		

MONEY AUTOBIOGRAPHY

Use the following questions to reflect on your personal experiences, feelings, and practices around money. You may write out the answers if you choose. During the workshop, you may choose how much you wish to disclose.

1. What was your first memory of money?
2. What was your happiest moment with money?
3. Your unhappiest?
4. How did you think about money as a child, teenager, young adult?
5. Did you feel poor or rich? Were you anxious about money?
6. What did your parents do to earn money?
7. Who handled the money in your family, and how?
8. Was money discussed in your family?
9. How did your family discuss and express generosity?
10. Did your parents trust you to go to the store to buy something?
11. Did you ever steal from your parents, other family members, or stores as a child?
12. How much money did your family have compared to your childhood friends?
13. Did you get an allowance?

14. How did your parents respond when you asked for something?
15. At what age did you start working?
16. Did you have to start working or did you want to start working?
17. What is the first money you recall earning and how did you earn it? How did you spend it?
18. When did you begin saving money?
19. Did anyone help you decide on a career based on how much money you wanted to make?
20. What messages did you get from your parents about career, earning money and spending money?
21. What was/is your view on money and dating? Who should pay for dates?
22. When did you get your first credit card? What were your feelings about it?
23. Will you inherit money? How does that make you feel?
24. Could you ask a close relative for a business loan? For rent/grocery money?
25. How do you feel about your present financial situation?
26. Do you know how much money you have right now? Do you know how much you owe right now?
27. Who handles the money in your current household, and how?
28. Is money easily discussed?
29. Is money abundant or scarce?
30. How does your family discuss and express generosity?
31. In what ways are you a good manager of money? In what ways are you a

poor manager of money?

32. Do you have a personal budget?
33. Have you made decisions concerning retirement, insurance, drafting a will, and so on?
34. What kinds of things do you buy on your credit card? Do you ever by groceries or necessities?
35. Do you make big purchases like cars, appliance or other expensive things with your credit card?
36. Do you know what interest rate you are paying and how much you owe?
37. Do you have any money secrets that you have never told anyone about?
38. Do you talk to your friends and family about money - how much you have or don't have, how much you make or how much they have and make?
39. How much money would you like to be making? What feelings does that bring up for you?
40. How do you feel about spending money on yourself?
41. Have you ever felt guilty about your prosperity?
42. How do you feel about the money situations of those who are more or less well-off than you?
43. How do you feel about begging? Welfare?
44. In what ways can you be generous? In what ways can you be stingy? Do you treat? Do you tip?
45. Do you give more than you receive or the reverse? Would others agree?

AUTHOR BIOGRAPHY

Eris Weaver is a facilitator, consultant, trainer, and public speaker known for her clarity, forthrightness, and humor. She became a facilitator because she has little patience for poorly run meetings.

Given how much of our work and community living time is spent in meetings, it is important that we make the best use of our precious time! Her most significant training ground for her work as a facilitator & communications consultant has been thirteen years with FrogSong, a cohousing community in Cotati, California.

Eris holds Masters degrees in Public Health and Library & Information Studies, both from University of California at Berkeley. Her previous professional life included community organizing and coalition building in a number of regional public health projects; managing health sciences libraries; teaching at the community college and adult school level; and serving on the board of several non-profits, including the Cohousing Association of the U.S. She is a member of the International Association of Facilitators and the International Forum of Visual Practitioners and a Fellow of the Leadership Institute for Ecology & the Economy.

She is deeply committed to the use of consensus and other cooperative decision-making processes to improve life within our communities and the world at large.

Her other passions include sea kayaking, surfing, running, yoga, dance, drawing, and costuming.

Eris can be contacted at eris@erisweaver.info or 707-338-8589.
Find out more about her services and workshops at www.erisweaver.info.